Days in Fall

Vic Parker

Raintree

Chicago, Illinois

© 2005 Raintree
Published by Raintree, a division of Reed Elsevier, Inc.
Chicago, Illinois
Customer Service 888-363-4266
Visit our website at www.raintreelibrary.com

Printed and bound by South China Printing Company.
07 06 05
10 9 8 7 6 5 4 3 2 1

Library of Congress Cataloging-in-Publication Data:
Parker, Victoria.
  Fall / Victoria Parker.
     v. cm. — (Days in)
Includes index.
Contents: It's fall — I spy in the park — Fall art — Let's go fly a
kite — Blackberry trip — It's Halloween — Beachcombing — At the fun
park — Helping in the garden — It's bonfire night.
  ISBN 1-4109-0738-4 (lib. bdg. : hardcover) — ISBN 1-4109-0743-0
(pbk.)
  1. Autumn—Juvenile literature. [1. Autumn.] I. Title.
  QB637.7 .P37 2004
  508.2—dc22
                              2003019848

Acknowledgments
The publisher would like to thank the following for permission to reproduce photographs: p. 4 Robert Harding Picture
Library (Andy Williams), pp. 6, 16 (Jeremy Bright), p. 14 (N. Penny); pp. 5, 7, 8, 9, 13 Trevor Clifford; pp. 10-11
Alamy/Leslie Garland Picture Library; p. 12 Reflections (Leslie Woodcock); pp. 15, 19, 17 Corbis; p. 18 Collections
(Nigel Hawkins); pp. 20, 21 Gareth Boden; pp. 22-23 Getty Images (Pauline Cutler)

Cover photograph reproduced with permission of Alamy/John Foxx

Some words are shown in bold, **like this**. You can find out
what they mean by looking in the glossary on page 24.

Contents

It's Fall!

In fall the leaves on many trees turn red and orange and brown.

4

What should you wear to go out?

5

I Spy in the Park

In the park the leaves make a colorful carpet.

6

What else has fallen
from the trees?

Fall Art

You can make bright fall pictures with leafprints.

Finished!

9

Let's go Fly a Kite

Fall winds are good for flying kites.

What shapes can you see in the sky?

Picking Berries

Let's pick **ripe** blackberries from the bush.

13

The Pumpkin Patch

Take a trip to the
pumpkin patch

You can choose
a big pumpkin.

It's Halloween!

It's fun to dress up in **scary**, spooky costumes for a Halloween party.

17

Back to School

School starts in fall.
How do you get to school?

You can paint a pretty
picture at school.

Helping in the Garden

It's time to plant **bulbs** in the garden.

They will grow into spring flowers.

There is lots of picking
up to do too!

Thanksgiving

Thanksgiving is a special day.

You can give thanks for your family.

23

Glossary

bulb a plant at rest before it sprouts and grows

ripe ready to pick or eat

Index

Notes for adults

The *Days in...* series helps young children become familiar with the way their environment changes through the year. The books explore the natural world in each season and how this affects community life and social activities. The books also focus on celebrations, which are particular to certain times of the year. Used together, the books will enable discussion about similarities and differences between the seasons.

This book introduces the reader to the season of fall. It will encourage young children to think about fall weather, wildlife and landscape and activities they can enjoy in fall. The book will help children extend their vocabulary, as they will hear new words such as *bulb* and *ripe*.

Additional information about the seasons

Not all places in the world have four seasons. Climate is affected by two factors: 1) how near a place is to the Equator (hence how much heat it receives from the Sun), 2) how high a place is (mountains are cooler than nearby lowlands). This is why some parts of the world have just two seasons, such as the hot wet season and the hot dry season across much of India. Other parts of the world have just one season, such as the year-long heat of the Sahara desert or the year-long cold of the North Pole.

Follow-up activities

- Make a collection of things you might find on an fall beach walk: a feather, a bit of driftwood, a smooth pebble, a pretty shell, etc.
- Take a trip to a library to find out more about Halloween and the fall festivals of other cultures.
- Make a pumpkin lantern for Halloween.